101 Facts About

PETS

101 Facts About

101 Facts About

TROPICAL FISH

Published by Ringpress Books Limited,
PO Box 8, Lydney, Gloucestershire,
GL15 4YN, United Kingdom.

Design: Sara Howell

Some photography courtesy of Tetra UK

First Published 2001
© 2001 RINGPRESS BOOKS LIMITED

ISBN 1 86054 153 4

Printed in Hong Kong through Printworks Int. Ltd.

0 9 8 7 6 5 4 3 2 1

101 FACTS ABOUT

TROPICAL FISH

Sarah Williams

Ringpress Books

1 Fish have been around for the last 400 million years. They are **aquatic vertebrates**. This means they are creatures with a backbone which live in water.

2 Most people keep freshwater tropical fish. Marine fish (those which live in salt water – left) are much more difficult to keep.

3 Altogether, there are more than 24,600 species (types) of fish. 8,000 of these are freshwater tropical fish.

4 Just like people, fish have five senses – sight, sound, smell, touch, and taste.

7 Scales do not have any colour. The bright colours of tropical fish are due to pigments (colours) in the skin, just underneath the scales.

5 Although they live underwater, fish need oxygen to breathe. They breathe through gills. Gills are vents which filter the oxygen out of the water.

8 Fish which are totally colourless or transparent (see-through), have no skin colour. The Glass Catfish (below) is a transparent fish.

6 The bodies of most tropical fish are covered with scales, made of a hard, bony material. They protect the fish from injury.

11 Some fish, such as the African Cichlid (below), are called **mouth brooders**. This means that the eggs hatch inside the fish's mouth! Until they are old enough to leave, the babies live in the mother's mouth – swimming out to play, and darting back inside if there is any danger.

9 Tropical fish divide into two groups: those which lay eggs (**egg layers**), and those which give birth to live young (**live bearers**).

10 Baby fish are called **fry**.

13 When the fish fills its swim bladder, it has to swim higher up in the water (closer to the surface). The fish can also empty this 'balloon', which allows it to sink to the bottom.

12 Tropical fish have a special organ inside them called the **swim bladder**. This is just like a balloon. When the fish breathes in, it can add some air to the balloon. Water is heavier than air, which is why anything filled with air floats.

7

14 All fish have fins. The size and shape of the fin can tell us a lot about the behaviour of that fish.

15 Flat or stocky fish, such as the Clown Loach (below), are designed to live on, or close to, the bottom.

16 Fish which are **streamlined** (have long, smooth bodies, to move easily through the water) and have long, pointed fins, are designed to live in open water. Swordtail fish (above) are like this.

17 Fish which are more slow-moving (e.g. the Oscar) tend to have rounded fins.

18 Each fin has a different way of helping the fish to move through the water.

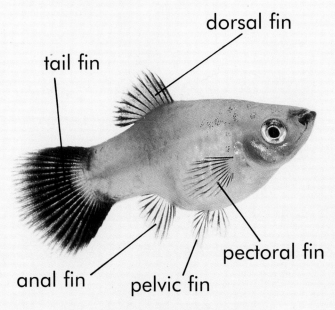

tail fin

dorsal fin

anal fin

pelvic fin

pectoral fin

19 The pectoral fins are close to the fish's head, next to the gills. They help the fish to balance, turn, and to swim backwards.

20 Pelvic fins come in pairs. They act as the fish's brakes.

21 Dorsal and anal fins are found at the back end of the fish. These fins help to keep the fish balanced.

22 The purpose of the tail fin is to push the fish forward. It may also help in turning and braking.

23 Fish need a lot of room to move around. They should not be kept in small fish bowls.

24 Choose the largest tank you can afford and can fit in your home. Glass tanks are better than acrylic (plastic) tanks because they are less likely to break.

25 Try to go for a long, rectangular tank, rather than a tall one. Fish tend to swim backwards and forwards in the tank, rather than up and down. A long tank gives them more room to move, and is easier to clean.

26 Tropical fish like warm water but need plenty of oxygen. The warmer the water, the less oxygen there is. Long aquariums allow more air to be absorbed into the water – helping the fish to breathe.

27 Normal furniture is not usually strong enough to support a full aquarium. Ideally, you should buy a purpose-made aquarium stand (right) for your tank.

28 Aquariums get very heavy when they are full. A 30-UK-gallon tank (36 US gallons/114 litres) will weigh about 250 pounds (114 kilos) when full.

29 Do not place the tank in direct sunlight or next to a radiator. The water can become too hot for the fish, and encourages the growth of **algae** (a type of fungus).

30 Fish have excellent hearing. It is best not to put the tank too close to a TV or hi-fi.

31 All aquariums should have a cover. This is known as the hood.

32 A hood prevents unwanted things from getting inside the tank, and also stops more gymnastic fish (ones which jump about a lot) from getting out!

33 The most important thing for keeping your fish healthy, is good, clean water. All aquariums should have a filter. This removes poisons from the water.

34 Water can be acidic or alkaline. Acids and alkalines are chemicals which can burn, but water dilutes them. Most of the time these chemicals are not strong enough to burn, but if your water is too acidic or too alkaline, it may hurt your fish.

37 Air stones are porous rocks that distribute (move around) the oxygen from the air pump, making sure that all the water in the tank is oxygenated.

35 The water in your aquarium can be tested, using a special kit called a pH measuring kit. You can buy one of these from any pet store.

38 Tropical fish like tropical temperatures. To keep the water warm, you will need a heater. You should also have a thermometer to check the temperature.

36 Filters add oxygen to the water, but it is still a good idea to have an extra air pump.

39 Tanks should have a fluorescent (extremely bright) light. This has the same effect on the fish as natural daylight. Tropical fish like 12 hours of daylight out of every 24 hours.

40 Some fish, such as Neon Tetra fish (below and left), reflect fluorescent light. If you look at one of these fish about an hour after you have turned out the lights, you will see that its bright strip has faded and it is almost see-through.

41 You will need gravel at the bottom of your fish tank. You should buy special aquarium gravel from your pet store. Natural gravel may pollute the water.

42 A good, pea-sized gravel is suitable for most fish. Pet stores sell it in lots of different colours.

43 Coral, although pretty, should be used for marine fish only – not freshwater tropical fish.

44 There are lots of decorations which you can add to your tank to brighten it up. 'Caves' and rock ledges will make your fish tank more like the fish's natural home.

45 You can have artificial or live plants in your tank. Plants make your aquarium more attractive for the fish. Live plants can also provide an extra source of food, but you must make sure that they are always healthy.

46 There are many different aquarium backdrops available. A backdrop is made of paper or plastic, and provides a 'scene' at the back of the aquarium.

47 After you have set up your tank, you will have to wait for at least ten days before adding any fish. This is because the water needs to mature (settle down) before it is right for the fish.

48 While your tank is maturing, you can choose your fish. There are 1,500 to 2,000 species of captive tropical fish from which to choose.

49 Each species of tropical freshwater fish belongs to a particular family of fish. These families are called **genera**.

50 The main families kept by tropical fish keepers are: catfish, cichlids, characiformes, cypriniformes, cyprinodonts, labyrinth fish, and rainbow fish.

51 Certain species and families should be kept together. This creates a balanced fish community.

52 Some fish form **schools**. This does not mean they have lessons! It means that they swim about in groups or **shoals**. If you buy a fish which schools, make sure you buy at least five or six of the same species.

53 Some fish, such as the Red Devil, can be aggressive. It is best to avoid hostile species in the aquarium, as they can fight and upset all the other fish.

56 The Clown Loach (below) grows up to be huge – 14 inches (35 centimetres) on average.

54 When some fish have an argument about territory, they kiss! Kissing is how fish mark the edge of their personal space. Peaceful fish which 'kiss' in this way are Kissing Gouramis (above).

55 Fish grow throughout their whole lives. Make sure you know how big each species can get before you buy it – you could get a nasty shock!

57 Make sure that all the fish you choose can live in the same range of temperature and in the same water conditions. Your pet store will advise you.

60 Inside an aquarium community, there are three sorts of fish: those which live at the top, those which live in the middle, and those which live on the bottom.

58 When you buy your fish, make sure the store is clean and cares for all its fish. Do not buy fish which have cuts or grazes.

61 Types of **top-dwelling** fish are: the Guppy, the Green Swordtail, the Black Molly, the Platy, the White Cloud Mountain Minnow, the Common Hatchetfish (below), and the Siamese Fighting Fish.

59 Any fish which has white spots (which are not usually part of its colouring), frayed fins, or dull skin, is unwell. Do not buy it.

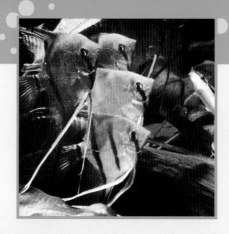

62 **Midwater** fish include: the Rosy Barb, the Red Rasbora, the Neon Tetra, the Angelfish (above), the Blue Gourami, and the Glass Catfish.

63 Types of **bottom-dwelling** fish are: the Clown Loach, the Red-tailed Shark, and the Synodontis Catfish (below).

64 Fish for beginners to avoid include the Green Discus, the Oscar, the Red Devil, the Jack Dempsey, the Tinfoil Barb, the Sucking Loach, the Red Snakehead, the Piranha and the Mudskipper.

65 After you have chosen your fish at the store, the owner will probably give you the fish in a plastic bag filled with water.

66 Make sure that plenty of oxygen has been pumped into the top of the bag, and try to keep the bag as steady as possible on the journey home.

68 Once the temperature of the water in the tank is the same as the water in the bag, add a handful of water from the tank to the bag. Then let the bag float for another 15 minutes.

69 Now add the fish to the tank by simply turning the bag upside down – gently!

67 Do not put the fish into the aquarium straight away. Instead, let the plastic bag float in the tank for 15 minutes (above). This allows the fish to become used to the temperature of the tank water.

70 When you choose your fish, make sure you know what foods they eat. Some fish are **carnivores** (they only eat meat), some are **herbivores** (they only eat plant foods), and some are **omnivores** (they will eat basically anything).

71 When you first start your aquarium, try to choose omnivorous fish. Their wide-ranging diet means they are far easier to feed.

72 The shape and position of a fish's mouth provide clues about what that fish eats.

73 Fish with upturned mouths (above) usually eat insects which live on the surface of the water.

74 Fish with forward-pointing mouths (below) usually live and feed in midwater.

22

75 Fish with down-turned mouths (right), usually live at the bottom of the water, feeding off creatures which live in the sand, soil, or plants.

76 Some fish, like the Suckermouth catfish (below), have huge sucker-like lips. These allow the fish to attach itself to a surface, and then the fish can browse the surface for food.

77 Other fish have **barbels** sticking out of their lips (above). These are rather like whiskers, and let the fish 'feel' the water and any food that might be in it.

78 Some fish have teeth. These are made of dentine, similar to human teeth.

79 The most famous, pointy-toothed fish is the Piranha (above). This fish is not an easy one to look after and is best left to the experts.

80 Unlike human teeth, fish teeth are always growing and being replaced. This means it does not matter if the teeth are broken or damaged.

81 It is a bit of a mystery why fish have teeth. Most do not seem to chew their food at all – often swallowing it whole.

82 The main part of your fish's diet should be made up of dried food (below). This contains all the things needed to keep your fish healthy. Two flakes per fish is about right in an average tank.

83 Dried foods come in flakes, pellets, or tablets. Most fish will be fine with flakes, but larger fish, or fish which live at the bottom of the tank, should be given pellets.

84 Give your fish different foods several times a week. They can get bored with flakes or pellets all the time. The fish below are feeding on a tablet food.

85 There are many household foods which are suitable for your fish. These include raw fish, raw meat, cooked potato, beans, peas, egg yolk, broccoli, cauliflower, chicken, uncooked spinach and lettuce (below).

food products from a pet store – some live foods have been known to make fish unwell.

86 If you give your fish any household food, you will need to chop it up quite small – to the same size as a food pellet – and only give them two to three lumps of it per fish.

87 Fish also like live food. Brine shrimp, earthworms, tubifex, whiteworms, and bloodworms can all be fed to your fish. You should always buy

88 Feed your fish over a five-minute period. Offer a little at a time and wait for it all to be eaten before you add more. Stop after five minutes.

89 Always feed your fish at the same time of day, and in the same spot in the tank.

90 Fish are greedy, and will eat as much as you can give them. Most have small stomachs, though. Did you know that a fish's stomach is roughly the same size as its eye? Never overfeed your fish (even if they beg) as it can make them seriously ill.

91 If you go away, fish can be left without food for up to three days. Any more than this, however, and you should either get someone to come in and feed them, or use an automatic food dispenser. This is a machine that feeds your fish for you.

92 Feeding is not the only chore which you need to do. Different checks are needed every day, week, month and year.

93 Every day, you will need to feed the fish, turn the lights on and off, and check the filters, temperature, and air pump.

94 Other regular tasks include: changing some of the water (10 to 20 per cent), vacuuming the gravel, feeding and trimming the plants, cleaning the inside of the tank glass with an algae scraper, and checking all the filter parts.

95 Once a year, the tank should be emptied. All the parts should be washed, and the filter parts should be changed. Make sure the water is the right temperature before you put your fish back in.

96 Fish do not like sudden changes of temperature. It can make them very ill and may even kill them.

97 Signs of illness are: rapid breathing, strange swimming patterns, lack of movement, and twitching or rubbing.

98 Loss of interest in food is one of the first signs of illness.

99 Sometimes it may be necessary to **quarantine** fish (keep them on their own). Keeping a hospital tank allows you to keep sick fish apart from the others.

100 If your fish become ill, ask your vet or your local pet store for help and advice.

101 If you look after your tropical fish well, they should remain healthy, look great in your home, and give you a fascinating hobby.

GLOSSARY

Algae: a fungus which grows inside the aquarium, which can harm the fish if it gets out of control.

Aquatic vertebrates: creatures that have a backbone and live in the water.

Barbels: fish 'whiskers'.

Bottom-dwelling: living at the bottom of the tank.

Carnivore: a meat-eater.

Egg layers: fish that lay eggs.

Fry: baby fish.

Genera: a family of fish.

Herbivore: a creature that only eats plants.

Live bearers: fish which give birth to live babies.

Midwater fish: fish that live in the middle depth of the aquarium.

Mouth brooders: fish that carry their babies in their mouths.

Omnivore: a creature that eats almost anything!

Pelvic fins: the fish's 'brakes'.

Quarantine: isolating a sick creature from the others, so that illness cannot spread.

School/shoal: a group of fish that swim around together.

Streamlined: a body which is long and smooth, allowing a fish to move through the water with very little effort.

Swim bladder: an organ inside the fish which allows it to swim higher or lower in the water.

Top-dwelling: living in the top part of the aquarium.

MORE BOOKS TO READ

All About Tropical Fishkeeping
Steve Windsor
(Ringpress Books)

Me and My Pet Fish
Christine Morley and Carole Orbell
(Two-Can)

*The Pet Owner's Guide to
Tropical Fishkeeping*
Mary Bailey
(Ringpress Books)

*ASPCA Pet Care Guides
For Kids: Fish*
Mark Evans and Roger A. Caras
(DK Publishing)

WEBSITES

Tropical fishkeeping
www.tropicalfishkeeping.com

All About Fish
www.geocities.com/mpreseau1/

Aquarists' guide
www.aquarist.net

AquariumFish.net
www.aquariumfish.net

To find more websites about tropical fishkeeping, use a good search engine to find one or more of these words: **tropical fish**, **aquariums**, **fishkeeping**.

INDEX